CREATE A SERVITOR
COMPANION

JOHN KREITER

Create a Servitor Companion

Dedicated to Harvey and Blue

Table of Contents

Author's Note 1

Introduction 3

Chapter 1: What Is a Servitor Companion? 9

Chapter 2: What Can a Servitor Companion Do? 19

Chapter 3: Get an Avatar/Fetish 25

Chapter 4: Charging Your Servitor Companion 33

Chapter 5: Control Your Servitor 43

Chapter 6: Maintenance and Care of Your Servitor Companion 55

Chapter 7: Create a Servitor Advisor 63

Chapter 8: Servitor Lover? 69

Chapter 9: Servitor Companion Room 83

Conclusion 91

Author's Note

Some people might find this book strange. It's going to ask you to play and to use your inner creativity and power to create a magical entity(s). A part of you might scream foul and demand that you computer mouse the heck out of this weirdness. Concepts that sound like "playing Pokémon", or like a "weird combination of quantum mechanics and witchcraft" will be presented. You have been warned.

Introduction

Here in the West we are very good at external manipulation. Our sciences are developed around incredibly powerful and practical ways to manipulate our external environment. Whether it is biology, chemistry, engineering, or even computer science, we have developed logical frameworks that allow us to manipulate objects and material within our physical world, in order to increase our awareness and empower ourselves.

This externally oriented world view has shown itself to be very successful in certain aspects. We can acknowledge the power of it when we look around and see all of the wonderful tools and other material constructs that make our lives so much more pleasurable and safe. Few though realize that this is but one possible world view, one that is based on the complete dominion of the external ego over personal beliefs. The external ego is very good at organizing our objective (physical) world but it has an incredibly limited perceptive ability. It thinks that the only real reality is the external one; only that which it can perceive through incredibly limited physical senses. As a result, it lives in a fearful and lonely world, surrounded by cold and indifferent objects, facing a life of decay and perpetual entropy.

The external ego believes (and because of its dominion over our modern lives, most of us believe) that the only way to get things done is through physical effort. It believes in a stark world where fun and play are a waste of time and therefore should be left to children. It glorifies that classic line "no pain, no gain", then in its quiet moments shakes with fear over what it believes to be its inevitable death as a purely physical organism, and whimpers as it contemplates its stark and painful existence.

There are some in the world though that believe that it is the internal that creates the external and that real manipulation of the objective/physical world begins through the manipulation of internal realities. These are old views (ones that are in many ways responsible for beginning the scientific era that now completely rules our lives here in the West) that allowed some to develop methodologies that enabled them to work with emotions, thoughts, and beliefs to alter external physical reality. These methodologies sometimes involved symbolism which can be represented through language, pictography, and even the manipulation of the senses. In the modern world we sometimes refer to these practices as magic(k), Witchcraft, the law of attraction, manifestation, sigil-craft, thought form creation, etc. In reality all of these methodologies are ways to work with the psyche; the belief being that any internal change (change to the psyche) is mirrored by external change (change to the physical world).

By its very nature, these methodologies understand that the external ego is not the absolute master that it perceives itself to be. Beyond this, this world view is better at supporting the external ego during its quiet moments, by showing it that it is not so alone. This world view can allow the external ego, to take a break sometimes from all of its tense control by showing it that all of those crazy emotions, impulses, and desires that it is perpetually trying to hold back have some purpose. That if this purpose is followed through creativity and play, it can discover a great power that it never knew it could access.

In this book we will explore some of these methodologies that take that 'internal to external' approach. We will plunge down the rabbit hole, and like Alice we will explore a Wonderland filled with magical and powerful creatures. This book is about having fun, about playing with your perceptions and your own mind in order to escape that cold ugly reality that the uneducated ego says is the only reality out there. Most importantly, this book is about discovering your true power, a power that will allow you to change every aspect of your life and get you many of the things you desire.

In my last book "Create a Servitor to Do Your Bidding", we explored some of this very powerful methodology of working with the 'internal to external'. That book showed you how to develop your personal power through servitors. There was a general focus but it was essentially geared towards the creation of worker servants; this book is the next step in that the powerful methodology.

You don't need to read the other book in order to practice the techniques that I will be showing you in this one. Everything that you need to know to create a servitor companion can be found here. In this book I will show you the next step in servitor creation. I will show you how to create a more specialized servitor that is more dynamic and has the potential to change your life forever. A servitor companion is a very powerful creature and a highly controversial one because it opens up aspects of our psyche that we here in the West like to suppress. Yet through the development, creation, and maintenance of a servitor companion you will begin to understand what true creation is really all about. With the techniques that you will learn in this book, you will be creating a very powerful servant that can greatly increase your happiness, creativity, talent, and pleasure. This book then is about changing your world from a drab and boring one, into an existence that is filled to the brim with adventure, joy, and personal satisfaction. In many ways this book is about true liberation; all in the comfort of your own home.

Even though the modern scientific revolution has promised us robots in every house, Artificial Intelligence, and Holodecks, we are not quite there yet. There is still a big gap between the incredible creativity of our inner psyche and the bleakness of lives that are only focused on the seeming harshness of our physical world.

Perhaps in this book you can learn a few things from old magicians and completely close that gap between our external scientific brilliance and our internal magical nature. Maybe we can have our cake and eat it too, as it were.

The Maya (as well as a number of other ancient civilizations) have a really interesting motif within their belief system which they call "the world tree". This tree represents the connection between heaven, the underworld, and physical reality. In a more intimate sense, this world tree also represents the bridge between internal subjectivity (the magical realms) and external reality; it is essentially the magical bridge of creation.

In this book you will be working with that bridge/process. You will see and experience the fountain of creation firsthand and you will understand how this is really the magical bridge that creates your entire reality. In this book I will show you a step-by-step procedure for creating a servitor companion; perhaps the greatest ally and cohort that you will ever have.

Chapter 1:
What Is a Servitor Companion?

If you have read my book, "How to Create a Servitor to Do your Bidding", then you will know that a servitor is a specifically created thought form that is designed to perform a personal task; an act of will/intent. A thought form then is a thought that is given enough attention or psychic energy so that it is able to manifest to a lesser or greater degree in what we consider consensual reality.

Servitors to me are an amazing thing; they allow us to truly begin to see the power of our conscious attention. Through the creation of thought forms, we are able to begin to understand the power of thoughts in a very literal way. We can begin to see how a thought begins to take form (that is, how it begins to take on form and substance within our physical world) which then allows it to have a superior ability to affect our reality.

As I had mentioned in my earlier book, thoughts are information units that can weave and meld with other thoughts using electromagnetic properties inherent within each of them. These thoughts can grow in strength as individuals and as gestalts through concentrated human psychic power. Human psychic power is focused attention, which can even be made more powerful when this focused attention is backed up by strong emotion.

At the moment of their inception, thoughts can be considered mental images or ideas. As the frequencies become more solid, in our opinion, thoughts could be considered something like emotions or emotion generating ideas. As the frequency of a thought comes closer to what we would consider physical reality, this thought could then be called a belief. Beliefs become assumptions and these assumptions soon become facts. Within short order, and under favorable conditions, facts become objects or events in what we call physical reality.

Creating and working with servitors means designing and manipulating these incredibly powerful by-products of human awareness called thoughts. Through concentrated attention, and the manipulation of our emotions and beliefs, we engage in the act of creating thoughts that are more potent than average ones. Using a type of ritualistic behavior, we focus our attention and our intention in order to create very powerful thoughts that can alter physical reality.

While in the book mentioned above, we focused on the creation of servitors to do our bidding, that is servitor's entrusted to perform different tasks, in this book we will be focusing on creating one particular type of servitor; one that is entrusted to be our companion, advisor, and perhaps even our lover if we so choose.

Task oriented servitors are designed in a way that makes their accomplishment of a particular task easier. What this means is that a servitor of this nature might have huge tentacles for example or it might have the ability to project some kind of light or energy. These traits, the physical design of our servitors as it were, make our servitors more capable.

A servitor companion needs to be designed with the same kind of forethought, but since its sole task is to keep us company, the design of the companion servitor is altered to suit this one task. A servitor companion is also a thought form that is designed and maintained differently because unlike task oriented servitors that we might not deal with for months at a time, a servitor companion can become a constant in our lives. A servitor companion has the possibility of being around us nearly all the time.

With that in mind then:

- Firstly, a servitor companion is not designed to be a worker; it is designed to be pleasing and entertaining. A servitor companion therefore is usually a lovely thing, a cute thing, a cool thing, a funny thing, sometimes even a wise thing, but it is definitely not the tool laden thought form that can sometimes have an almost Frankenstein like appearance. A servitor companion is designed to make you happy and must therefore be very pleasing to your eye.
- Secondly, a servitor companion is charged in a completely different way than the worker servitor. You will most likely want your companion servitor with you on a regular basis and will therefore be dealing with your servitor in a very personal way. Because of this relationship the way you charge and go about maintaining your servitor is completely different.

In many ways a servitor companion is a thought form that needs to attain a more physical vibration. What I mean by this is that first and foremost you must be able to see this companion clearly. Over time you will also be able to feel and hear this companion; you might even be able to experience your servitor with your other two senses as well. In other words a servitor companion needs to become as real as possible to you personally.

Over time, as you charge your servitor companion and as you continue charging it through your interactions with it, your thought form will attain a type of thickness. Now this thickness has nothing to do with physical width, this thickness is an internal aspect that can best be described as an increase in probable action. Remember that you are dealing with thoughts here, and they do not follow the physical laws that we are all used to. Thoughts are continually growing and developing just like living creatures in the physical world but they don't need to increase in size and mass in order to do so. A thought can be said to increase in size internally like for example an intellect can increase in size without changing the size of its container (the brain); it grows in complexity not in dimension.

This internal increase in your thought form, through your attention and charging, increases the complexity of the thought form, which essentially means that it increases the probable potential of this servitor. Think of it like a network; the more attention and charging that you give your companion, the more complex that this internal network becomes. Let's say for example that your servitor started with the network connection from one point to another, through your efforts and your charging, it will develop different points so that instead of having a 2 point network connection, it will develop a 3 then a 10 and then perhaps even 100 point connection; so that over time the network connection that makes up the basis of your companion servitor will be highly complex indeed.

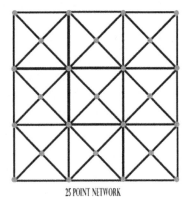

2 POINT NETWORK   5 POINT NETWORK   25 POINT NETWORK

Now, this internal complexity which I describe as a network or as probable potential is what will eventually give your companion thought form a type of sentience. True sentience will never be possible of course because your servitor will never have the ability to choose its actions, but what this internal probability potential will do is to give it a type of normal 'life like' behavior which you will be able to identify with. As a result of this identification, a bond between you and your companion will be created.

I know that this sounds complicated but you don't really need to understand all this in order to create a very good companion servitor. I mention this here because I believe that you are interested in learning about thoughts and their potential and because I wish to do my due diligence in giving you a good background as to why you are doing what you are doing and how this affects yourself and your creation.

If you are having problems understanding this network connection that I have mentioned, think of it like you forming a bond with a human friend. You meet someone and finding them pleasing, you try and strike up a friendship. To do that, you begin to talk about different subjects that interest you and begin to pay attention to see if some of these subjects are also interesting to your potential friend. If you are both interested in sailing let's say, then there is an internal aspect within you that is very similar to an internal aspect within your potential friend. This then becomes a connection from one network (you and your love of sailing) to your friends network (him and his love of sailing), and through this internal connection between the both of you, a bond is formed.

As you charge and interact with your companion servitor, you are essentially feeding it these internal aspects of yourself which increase the complexity of your servitor and make it easier for you to develop a connection with it over time. A servitor does not have a pre-existing network like a human friend, so part of what you are doing with it when you charge and interact with it is to create a network of your own design.

These internal aspects that you feed into your servitor companion are indeed a type of probability potential because just as a network increases in complexity, the development of these internal aspects allow your companion the potential of acting in unique probable ways. A simple thought form network can go from A to B and that's it, a more complex thought form could go from A to C or B, a truly complex thought form could go from A to D to

M to Q to Z. Beyond this, this network can be accessed not just from one point to another in order to create one action, this network can also grow in complexity in that it can access a number of different network points in order to create a new event; for example instead of just going from A to B, it could go from A to Q to M to R to D, and then finally to B. In this way the final outcome becomes different, and truly novel behavior can be created by your servitor.

Unique behavior like this is very pleasing to the mind and it is what will allow your companion servitor to become a great source of entertainment for you. As your servitor grows and makes you happy through its seemingly random action, a bond will be created between the both of you. Your love of your new friend will empower it and in many ways it could be said that your servitor companion will seek ways to increase the love and happiness that you feel. This bond and happiness will grow with each interaction.

Eventually your servitor companion will become very real to you. There will come a time when you will no longer need to strain to see and feel your servitor companion, when it will begin to do things that you did not expect; this is when the magic truly begins.

I know that this can also sound a bit creepy. In many ways this concept can mirror our Frankenstein phobia; with our great development in technology we have begun to consider the possibility of having robotic friends and workers. With these new contemplations, people also contemplate the possibility that something could go wrong and that these machines could rise up against us. So it was, with magicians of old, that they too thought that these thought forms created with their minds, these magical creations, would also rise up somehow against them. Many live in mortal dread of evil things that lurk in the dark, but they do so because they do not understand the extent of their personal power and as a result don't have the knowledge to deal with thought forms and other entities that can be bothersome at times.

In this book you will realize that the servitor companion can be designed any which way you like and that it will never rise up against you in any way as long as you take responsibility for your own psyche. I will show you how to maintain a proper relationship with your servitor companion and I will also show you how to punish and even destroy this servitor companion if it comes to it. But it won't come to this because it doesn't have to; you are far more powerful than you think you are. As a true creator, you are here to refine your power and creative potential through joy, happiness, and play. Think of servitor companions as the next step in your internal evolution.

Chapter 2:
What Can a Servitor Companion Do?

A servitor companion is a friend, an ally. It is a more complex version of the imaginary friend that children sometimes have when they are growing up. If you can remember back to your childhood then you will most likely remember many times when you engaged in a complex game where you created a number of people in order to make your game more exciting. For example, you could play being ship captain in which case you most likely created an entire crew so that you could boss them around. Some children even engaged in creating one individual friend, a special someone, whom they would constantly interact with, a very special creation that they used for companionship and support.

Don't think that you are some kind of poor social misfit because you are contemplating creating an imaginary friend. The fact of the matter is that we are constantly creating people like this in our dreams and it is actually a quite complex mental action that is incredibly beneficial to our psyche. In the dream state, these mental creations help us a great deal because they allow us to interact and to see possibilities and probabilities from many different perspectives. The ability to create a servitor companion therefore is a sign of a powerful and complex intellect.

(Please note though that not all dream characters are mental creations).

A servitor companion then is a very complex imaginary friend. The term 'imaginary' has both positive and negative aspects when trying to understand what a servitor companion really is. In my opinion it has positive connotations in that it is through this definition that we can see that this thought form that we are creating is being imagined into existence; it comes from the mind and is an internal thought that we are bringing into a more concrete physical presence. The term 'imagination' has negative connotations though because of the fact that most people believe the imagination to be such a powerless aspect of our reality. Children can use the imagination as much as they want, they don't have to pay the bills after all, but grown-ups should not be playing with their imagination, grown-ups are supposed to grow up.

But as you might already know, if you have created a servitor in the past, thoughts and the imagination are far from powerless. Properly directed human attention and imagination can make these thoughts more 'concrete', and through their proper direction they can be made to effect consensual reality. Thoughts are not ethereal wispy little things that flow constantly in your mind. They are the true bedrock of what we call reality, and true physical action is thought manipulation. As such, a servitor companion is not an imaginary friend; it is a true concrete entity that is designed for personal happiness and support. This is probably the biggest secret on this planet; true power comes from thought control and manipulation.

As your servitor companion grows in strength and complexity, it will begin to take on its own characteristics. What I mean by this is that your ethereal companion will essentially develop a personality. Remember the growth in the network connections that I spoke of in the last chapter; as these grow, the complexity of your servitor will grow and therefore the personality of your companion servitor will also grow and develop. You will see this in odd little quirks that will develop in the personality of your companion. For example it could be the case at your companion might start to like cats and as you pay attention to this love of felines, your companion will develop a whole branch of its personality devoted to its love and its interaction with the cats in your life.

As you charge and interact with your servitor companion more and more, you will be tempted at times to give it certain tasks. A servitor companion can become very real, over time you will be able to see it without struggle and you will be able to touch it and interact with it in a completely natural way. It will then feel quite right to give it a certain task, since you really could not ask for a better and more powerfully created thought form. My suggestion to you is that you do not act on these feelings.

The reason for this is that whenever you create a servitor and then give it a task, this servitor becomes irreparably changed by the task that it is given. If for example you create a servitor to defend your home, then this servitor will take on many traits that are required in order to become a great defender. A defender sometimes needs to be aggressive and most often it needs to be incredibly stubborn. The more that these traits develop within this servitor, the better it is because then this servitor becomes that much better at doing its job; these traits though are not good traits for your servitor companion to have for obvious reasons.

A servitor companion should be created to bring you happiness and joy, perhaps even to make you laugh. Make sure that you keep it focused on this one goal.

A servitor companion then is created to keep you company when you are lonely. If you travel a great deal by yourself, then it can travel with you and support you when you are feeling low. It is first and foremost a real creature that can help you in many ways but the fact that it is fundamentally a thought form means that it has a flexibility that comes in really handy sometimes. It can be put away when it is not needed, and it can even be forgotten and put away forever when you choose. It takes up no space per se, you don't have to feed it, and you don't (or should not) worry too much if you hurt its feelings. A servitor after all is a servant, it is up to you to decide how you treat it and what you will do with it.

A servitor companion is the perfect friend in many ways because it is never needy. A servitor companion can develop certain personality traits that might make it seem like it is needy at times but this is just a part of its growing complexity. Servitors do not have desires so the neediness is hollow; it is just an aspect of growing complexity. This complexity is developed through a fine tuning by your psyche as it cultivates characteristics within your thought form that it finds funny or appealing in some way. Think of yourself as a gardener; you can choose to grow a certain type of flower and you can even change some characteristics of this flower if you want. When you are tired of this flower you can grow another and let this one wither or if you want you can grow a carrot instead. It's your garden to do as you like, if you are tired of gardening you can turn around and walk away or you can till the whole garden and put in a parking lot.

Remember always that you are the master and it is the servant. All you have to do is to learn how to treat it properly and manage it; you will discover more on this in the chapter on 'controlling your servitor'.

Yes, a servitor companion can be designed so that it becomes your ethereal lover. As such they can take any shape you want and any attitude that you desire. It can be told to leave whenever you desire without guilt or recriminations. It is the perfect companion and one that we all have the right to create and keep without guilt or fear.

In this modern world where we are all becoming more and more separate thanks to the incredible growth in information technology, a servitor fills a need for companionship and adventure that many of us are wanting. In a cyber age full of computer generated creations, the servitor companion seems only fitting. It is an old technique, it is a nearly lost human skill, and it is one that will allow you to discover an infinite world of possibilities.

Chapter 3:
Get an Avatar/Fetish

Since we will be creating a specific type of servitor, we can refine these techniques to suit the requirements of that specific being. A servitor companion is a very special type of servitor which is highly dependent on image; how it looks and how it feels. We can then say that its image is all important. Its job after all will be to relate to you personally and for this you need to have a servitor that is highly pleasing to your senses.

In the development and charging of this creature, you will need to pay very close attention to its physical detail and to its image in general. As you do so, you will realize that the feeling that you have towards this servant is directly related to its image. When you see something pleasing, something that truly inspires you visually, you will notice that you feel good. It is this internal pleasure that you must pursue when you are developing the image of your servitor.

Also as this internal pleasure develops, through the beauty of this creature's image, you will realize that there is also a direct link between internal feelings and external ones. As you develop and go about charging your servitor, you will most likely wish to touch your creation. Your companion must be a pleasure to your senses; to that end you must put extra effort into coming up with the best imagery for this creature possible. I therefore recommend that you get yourself an avatar/fetish.

avatar: an icon or figure representing a particular person in computer games, Internet forums, etc.

AND

fetish: an inanimate object (or image) worshiped for its supposed magical powers or because it is considered to be inhabited by a spirit.

If you combine the definitions above, you will get a rough idea of what I'm talking about when I ask you to get yourself an avatar/fetish. I suppose there is now a need to come up with a new definition for an avatar/fetish, because this is truly what you will be looking for and what you will be using to create your servitor companion.

An avatar/fetish therefore, in relation to what we will be accomplishing in this book:

is an icon (sometimes even a file of images) or figure that represents a particular servitor companion. It is used to develop the form and feel of a subjective entity and as such can become the home of this servitor companion if you wish. It is the clay mold upon which your companion is made.

Here then is where the fun part begins because your first task is to find the perfect avatar/fetish. To do this I recommend that you scour your internal feelings and your external world until you find an image that fills you with joy. Many of us in this modern world are filled with great amounts of beautiful imagery thanks to our cyber culture and the many, many characters that dwell within it. Give yourself free reign and explore your world until you find the perfect image, the perfect avatar, the perfect fetish, for the development of your new servant companion.

If you are a manga enthusiast, then might I suggest that you look for a character that you find most pleasing and turn this into your avatar/fetish. These Manga characters often have collectible plastic dolls that are the perfect avatar fetish, but you don't need to have a physical object like a doll; a file of images or photographs will do just as well. If you want then, you can look up a manga character that you truly enjoy and with the help of one very strong image or a combination of them, you can use these quite successfully as your avatar/fetish.

But don't focus your entire search in the manga world, if you are interested in Celtic mythology for example, and would like to have a medieval Dragon as your servant companion, then browse the extent of your world for either a simple doll, or that perfect image online that captures the creature that you would like to bring to life.

If you wish, you can also use a stuffed creature or toy as an avatar fetish. Many children start this process of creating a thought form companion by using toys like a stuffed bunny, and some end up doing it quite successfully. Pleasurable fun toys like these are truly an extension of deeply felt inner feelings and thoughts. Their beauty and imagined traits represent powerful ideals that children can aspire to as they play. In the West we tend to set harsh limits on these iconic figures, we label them as toys for children and look down upon grown-ups that still like to 'play' in this fashion, but you should realize that these are highly prejudiced restrictions imposed by a highly controlling external ego that fears a loss of control.

In the East, especially in Japan, there is no taboo associated with the exploration of this rich creative aspect within all of us. As a result, people in many of these countries are able to explore an unbelievably rich inner reality, a reality that makes them incredibly creative, emotionally stable, and far better at dealing with stark and difficult life conditions.

Fortunately the West is seeing a resurgence in this internal exploration of toys and games for adults. The video game world is reviving our creative inner realities and the popularization of comic books is allowing us once again to explore the deep relation between imagined superheroes (our ideals and values) and the full pantheon of old pagan gods and nature spirits. A little stuffed rabbit or a cool star wars action figure can be used as a wonderful avatar/fetish therefore, and as long as you are willing to put in the time to charge your servitor companion properly. Even the most intricate doll can be given concrete etheric form.

You will be spending a lot of time with this creature if you are successful in your endeavors, I therefore implore you to choose wisely and try and find some avatar/fetish that you will be happy with for a while. If you are a talented artist, then you can certainly draw or create your own avatar/fetish and you will become that much closer to your imagery because of your creative efforts. You can truly see the creation of a servitor companion as the next step in the artistic desire to objectify those internal images and feelings within. An artist brings to life internal feelings and images that come from deep within their souls. The creation of a servitor companion is the next step in this creative process since it begins to truly objectify and give life to those internal feelings and images that you have brought forth from your inner world.

Above all things always do remember though that this is a fun process. It is like a child's game taken to the next level, and just like a child's game, it must be fun and must come from within as a feeling of joy, excitement, and play. You will know what your perfect avatar/fetish is because it is the one thing that will bring you great joy, and to look for this image, or to develop this image on your own, you must pursue this joy. Make it fun, not serious. Let your mind go and explore your own inner desires.

Your avatar/fetish is a private thing. It is quite possible that if, for example, you get yourself some kind of doll as your avatar/fetish that you might want to mount it somewhere where others might see, but this does not mean that you have to tell them that this is an extension of an actual existing thought form. This magical endeavour is your secret and you must always keep it as such because the minds of others can sometimes be intrusive; their intent/desire is not your intent/desire. This magical endeavor must be free from the judgment of others.

If you want to, you can keep your avatar/fetish hidden somewhere and only take it out when you need help in developing and identifying with your servitor companion. Never though believe that this avatar/fetish is some kind of supremely special object that needs to be taken care of. It is but a tool to an end, that end being the creation of the perfect thought form of your desires. If for example, your avatar/fetish is destroyed for some reason, then do not fear for your servant companion because there is no critical attachment between one and the other; one is just used as a physical prop in order to allow you to bring to life a mental creation. An avatar/fetish is a tool and a prop to help your mind create and work on an image in 3 dimensional space.

My personal recommendation to you is that you stay away from people you know or people that you have known when you are looking for your avatar/fetish. There is no dark and evil reason for my request. There is not some kind of inherent danger in creating an avatar/fetish from a deceased person for example. I recommend that you stay away from people you know because there can be complications when it comes to the development of your relation with your servitor companion. The reason for this is that people that you know personally already hold a huge part of your mind, that is they have already created a very strong network pattern within your psyche, and this large network is a complicated one full of many emotions and beliefs.

When you create a servitor companion, you want something fresh. You require a new beginning and a road that leads towards pure pleasure, without the complications of a human relationship. A servitor companion is supposed to be fun. Interaction with this servant that you are creating must become a simple and joyful affair and not a complicated one where you resurrect old demons from past displeasures and recriminations. Let your avatar/fetish therefore be something that gives you a feeling of utter joy with no complications. Your servitor companion should be light, airy, happy, wholly egoless, a servant to please you in any way you desire. With this in mind, choose your avatar/fetish with great discrimination and only settle when you find the most pleasurable image or form, an image or form that brings you great happiness and makes you long to have a creature like this become part of your life.

Chapter 4:
Charging Your Servitor Companion

Before we begin learning about the charging process, I do think that it is a good time to review the relative length of the servitor creation process (about 3 days for a servitor worker and 2 to 4 weeks for a servitor companion) and why the development and creation of powerful thought forms, is so worth it:

Some might argue that this is a long and somewhat complicated methodology. I personally don't think so and if you have any experience meditating or even physically exercising for a segment of time every day, you won't find it very hard at all. Some people though get frustrated and usually mention a number of different techniques that use far less effort to supposedly get similar results. While every person is different and it could be that some are more suited to using different methods, I can tell you that working with thought forms is infinitely more powerful than working with many of the methods typically expounded by modern magick and Law of Attraction practitioners. The reason for this is that thought forms bridge the gap between the objective and the subjective world and are in that regard a self-empowering exercise that compounds all psychic and manifestation work. Even when you are working with sigils, you are essentially just working with the type of focused intent that is then given extra powers through focused attention. Any ritual that you do in order to create these sigils or the like is just a way to be able to focus your attention and therefore your psychic energy in a more powerful way.

As powerful as any of these methods or rituals are, you are still essentially working with a two-dimensional system at best. With a powerful thought form (or servitor) on the other hand, you are taking an extra step by first bringing your incantation/spell/ritual into three-dimensional reality, giving it intent (or you might say an inbuilt desire to fulfill itself by accomplishing your bidding) and then sending it out to manifest your desires.

So as powerful as a sigil or other similar rituals might be, they will never have the potency of the thought form. As powerful as a manifestation method could be, it will never have the same concentrated force that a servitor can have. While some might believe that a thought form like this could end up complicating your manifested desires and perhaps bringing more trouble than they are worth, in actuality the exact opposite is true. It is far easier to create a poorly developed sigil or pictogram, and it is usually these methodologies that end up bringing you what you want through complications. A servitor can be developed and maintained very much like a machine and unlike typical manifestation techniques, the more you use it the more powerful it becomes.

This power and precision have a price though, the price is that you will have to put in extra effort and dedicate more time to create a powerful machine that can then truly give you exactly what you desire. It essentially means that you will need to manifest a servant before you manifest what you desire. But this act of servitor manifestation helps to show your mind what it is capable of and as a result, even greater manifestations are possible. Working with servitors increases your confidence and therefore increases your psychic potency. This is essentially then a self-empowering loop!

Now back to charging your servitor companion

Since image and feeling are so important, this is what we must focus on when we charge our servitor companion. Unlike the worker servitors that I discussed in my previous book, where I had you focus on your logo or sigil briefly in order to bring life to your creation, the servant companion must be created through a deep focus on your avatar/fetish. Since the servitor companion is all about image, you might say that it is the courtesan of the servitor world.

What you are going to be doing when you charge your servitor companion is to try and bring your avatar/fetish to life as a separate 3 dimensional etheric form. For the charging process therefore, your avatar/fetish is most important and will be constantly used as a reference in order to help you bring your servitor to 3 dimensional life. The avatar/fetish is the original stamp that you will use to focus your visualizations and your attention.

Unlike a regular servitor you will not be using the method of three powerful bursts of intensely focused belief as a charging method. To charge your companion you will need to use a slower method that will allow you to focus the depth of your mind into a highly detailed image of this creature.

The Process:

1. To begin the charging process, I want you to find a quiet room, one where you will not be disturbed for 15 minutes to half an hour. In that room I want you to put your avatar/fetish before you and I want you to spend this time studying it as closely as possible. Take this time to try and memorize all the features of your avatar/fetish so that if you close your eyes you will be able to remember every single detail.

There might be some flaws in your avatar/fetish. That is it might not be the perfect image or doll of the servitor companion that you want to create. Do not worry about this for now, just focus on remembering those aspects of your avatar/fetish that you want to re-create in your servitor. I suggest that you do this for a week, or for as long as you think it takes for you to memorize this avatar/fetish completely. For some people this will not be a long process and for others it might be a longer period depending on how good your memory is. It is up to you to decide how long you wish to spend on this step.

2. When you believe that you have memorized this avatar/fetish so that you can close your eyes and see it quite easily, I want you to begin the second step in the charging of your servitor. Once again go into this quiet room where you will not be disturbed for 15 minutes to half an hour. If you can, try to darken the light in this room as much as possible, but try to keep one source of low light focused on your avatar/fetish. Some might want to put their avatar fetish on top of a small table beside a candle in the corner of their dark and quiet room. This would be ideal but I would not do this if it brings up odd connotations for you. What I mean by this is that some people tend to equate dark rooms and candles with dark magic and this can be a psychological hang up that can be a hindrance for some.

Do realize that this is not a dark and evil ritual, it is just the most efficient set-up to obtain a desired result. For those that enjoy a more Gothic reality, this could be the perfect set up; it is up to you to decide how best to proceed on this. There is no reason why you could not use a flashlight or colored lights of some kind if you wish to. My only reason for wanting you to create this atmosphere is that this set-up will make it much easier for you to focus your attention on the avatar/fetish and visualize with the least amount of hindrance possible.

Once you have your quiet room set up perfectly, I want you to try and visualize your servitor companion with your eyes closed. I want you to spend 15 minutes to half an hour in this darkened room with your eyes closed, and I want you to try and see your servitor companion before you in your mind's eye. In many ways this should be an act of memory recall for you, but I want you to tell yourself that you are now creating your servitor companion; I want you to tell yourself that you have begun the process , this visualization that you are doing now in your mind's eye is beginning the process of creating this creature. This personal statement given to your self is a statement of intent, and as such it will color the way that you approach this new visualization time; it will quite literally change your energy and focus.

I suggest that you continue with this exercise for about a week, or as long as you think it will take for you to be able to visualize your servitor companion clearly with your eyes closed. Follow your intuitions on this and make sure that the image in your mind of your servitor companion is as perfect as you can make it.

3. The third step in charging your companion is to spend 15 minutes to half an hour in this darkened room trying to visualize your servitor companion with your eyes open. What I mean by this is that you will now try to visualize your servitor in the room with you. Try to visualize your servitor companion floating in the darker part of the room in which you find yourself so that at one end you will have your well-lit avatar/fetish and at the other side of the room you will be visualizing your true servitor companion thought form. Try to recreate every single detail of your avatar/fetish in this thought form that you are creating; try to see the avatar/fetish floating on the other side of the room. Thanks to the time that you spent memorizing and recalling the image of your companion in your mind, and thanks to the fact that you are in a dark room, this should be relatively easy for you.

Do remember that you are trying to create every single aspect of this avatar/fetish so make sure that your visualized servitor companion spins around sometimes as you visualize it so that you add form not only to the front part of it but to the back and sides as well. Practice visualizing your servitor companion from every angle, do this until you can clearly see it floating around the room, spinning maybe, until the visualizations of your companion is perfect. Do this for as long as it takes; for some it could take a week and for others it could take a couple. Follow your intuitions on this as with everything else, but make sure that the visualization of your servitor companion is the best possible.

4. In the fourth step of your charging, I want you to try and start moving and interacting with your servitor. In this step of the charging process, I want you to bring more life into your thought form. You do this by visualizing your servitor moving around in a more natural manner. For example if your avatar/fetish is a doll, imagine that it's not frozen like your avatar/fetish but that it's limbs are moving and it is looking around like a living creature. Have it come towards you and then move away, have it turn around and perhaps walk in the air, have it flap its wings if it has wings.

As it develops and you feel comfortable with your visualizations, you can even try talking to it and imagine it responding in whatever way you wish it to. At this stage you might even want to visualize touching your companion; you do this by imagining that you are extending a hand (a type of etheric hand or your actual hand) and you are caressing your servitor. Feel its hair/fur, its armor, its scales, its soft skin, its lustrous form. Feel your companion servitor with your etheric hand or real hand until your visualizations feel very realistic; as real as touching a physical object. This type of ultra-realistic visualization is far easier than you may think, it just takes a little practice.

This step truly brings your servitor companion to life so you must devote as much time as possible on this step. I recommend a week on this step, but the true judge is your own subjective feelings. At the end of this step, your companion must feel real. It will also seem to act like a real living thing, and it must seem very real to you; for as long as you are visualizing it in this private room.

5. The fifth and final step in the charging of your servitor companion does not take as long as the other steps but it is an emotionally intense process. Once in your quiet room, focus your attention on your avatar/fetish. Now look to the other corner of this darkened room and visualize your servitor companion. Imagine that it is interacting with you and it is moving around in a natural fashion; as you do so slowly repeat your companion's secret name three times.

After each repetition of your companion's name, I want you to feel with every ounce of your being that this servitor companion before you is real and it is therefore alive. Play with your own beliefs here and try to feel with every fiber of your being that this thought form is now real and alive.

On the third and last repetition of the name, I want you to focus all your attention and effort in believing with every single ounce of your being that your servitor is there now alive. Feel this vividly, feel it being alive, know that it is alive with all your being, with every single ounce of your will. Do this for 5 to 10 minutes. This is an intense exercise, believing something with your entire being might even make you sweat with the effort, so don't be surprised if this happens. Just keep focusing on your one goal, on your one feeling without stopping for the full 5 to 10 minutes.

When you are done, in a loud and commanding voice say, "(servitor's name) you are alive!"

Now your servitor is a real thing, to be called forth whenever you mention its name. Your servitor companion is now alive and fully charged and you can begin to interact with it as you desire. Depending on how well you visualized and how much effort you made in your final charge in step 5, this will now be a powerful thought-form indeed and it will begin to interact with you if you let it.

If you interact with your servitor companion on a regular basis, then you will not need to formally recharge it again since each interaction will recharge this thought form. As you develop a friendship with your servitor, your interactions will become more pleasurable because you won't need to focus very hard to see and even feel your servitor companion. If you are having problems getting to this point (where you can easily see and interact with your companion) then it is most likely because there is a part of you that still doubts its existence. If this is the case then might I suggest that you take this wonderful quote to heart:

"What we need to do to allow magic to get hold of us is to banish doubts from our minds. Once doubts are banished anything is possible."
— Don Juan

Chapter 5:
Control Your Servitor

Even before its final charging, I am certain that you will realize that you have an incredible creature at your disposal. After its final charge, you can start interacting with this servitor companion that you have created and if you have properly defined this creature's imagery and therefore some pleasing aspects of its character, you can begin to interact with a companion that for all intents and purposes is alive and is here now ready to please you in any way that it can.

To interact with your new servitor companion, you will most likely begin by calling it to you. This is the first step in interacting with it after all; calling it to you and allowing it to materialize before you.

Once you do call it to you, you might find that it won't be as physically crystal clear as you might like. Don't worry about this as this will fix over time as you interact with it more and more. That is, your servitor will become more and more physically real the more that you interact with it, so don't be discouraged if at first you find it difficult seeing it clearly without intense concentration on your part. The more you interact with it, the less you will have to make an effort to see it and play with it.

After you have summoned it to you, you will want to begin to start a relationship with it; to do this I recommend that you talk to it. Call it by its name and share funny stories with it, or ask it to do certain things for you. Through your interactions you will start to develop a certain inner sense, you could even call it a little voice that you can sense deep within yourself. This voice is actually your servitor companion's voice and as you interact and talk with it you will begin to realize that through this intuition (inner voice), you will be able to understand what it is saying to you.

For example you might ask your servitor a question and after you do so you might get a sense deep within yourself of what your servitor might say. This intuition as to your servitor's reply is actually part of your servitor's response. If you listen to this voice and you allow it to expand, it will permit communication to begin between you and your servitor companion. Over time this communication will flow effortlessly just like a regular conversation; it might actually flow faster since after a while you might not even want to speak but just interact with your servitor through your mind. A flow of communication like this can be hilarious, I personally can have conversations with my companion/familiar that have me laughing and smiling almost instantly.

After you have summoned it, and you begin to have a communication with it, you might want to ask it to do different things for you. You might want it to go across the room or to perform a certain trick for you in order to delight you. If for example your servitor companion is a beautiful human like creature then you might want to have it dance for you, or if your companion is a small Dragon for example, you might wish to have it fly around the room for you. Having a magical creature like this fly around a room in your house is an awesome thing.

Some people have a huge problem here. They think that to have an imaginary, in your mind, creature supposedly flying around your room like this is pure delusion. But this is classified as delusion only because you are supposedly tricking yourself into seeing this being. There is a point though, when you have charged your 'thought form' properly, when you are no longer tricking yourself as it were, when you are no longer making an effort to see this thing. Then, at that moment, things change, the world changes!

Now, from the very beginning of this relationship that you are now developing with your companion, you must make sure that you place yourself firmly as the master. This can be a very difficult subject for some so I will put it in bold letters for you;

You have created a servant companion, you have not created a partner.

What this means is that you must never let your creation act like it is the creator. Some people find this difficult, they have friends and relatives that are usually telling them what to do and find it impossible to conceptualize a situation where they are the ones calling the shots. It is even the case that some people can't ever develop a relationship where they are dominant. When people like this have pets, even their pets end up telling them what to do.

If you can honestly say that you are a person with this kind of problem then I suggest that you think hard before you create a servitor companion. In order to work with thought forms and to master your mind in general, you will need to develop a very strong intent or will. This does not mean that you will have to change your ways and become some kind of bully that tells everyone else what to do, but it does mean that you will need to take charge of your own mind and never let yourself be swayed or bullied into anything; at least not when it comes to your work with thought forms and your servitor companion.

To make it simple, think of it this way:

You are the master, you are superior. You are the creator and leader of your creations; they are lesser than you and must always bow to your will. You then loosen their leash a little bit when it pleases you but they must forever be in your control. You are not dealing with an equal, you are dealing with a servant. If you can maintain that posture in your mind but at the same time have fun with your companion and let it grow in a natural and loving way, then you can truly master all your thought forms and will never have any trouble with any of your creations.

If you have read my other book on creating servitors then you probably know that I have always recommended that you watch a few episodes of the show," The Dog Whisperer". In this show Cesar Millan shows people how to interact with their pet dogs and how to create the correct attitude and relationship with them. This is truly the best show for anyone engaging in the act of creating thought forms because it tells you so much about creating alpha dominance and becoming a pack leader as opposed to being controlled and manipulated by your creations. In the show, Caesar usually has to show people how their pets have taken over their lives and are now kings of the castle. He tells people how to identify the signs of the dominating dog and how to correct this behavior through an assertive and dominant stance that is powerful and unshakable but not highly aggressive, emotional or angry. If you are able, I do recommend that you watch a few of these episodes if you can; you can probably watch enough for free on YouTube. Study his techniques because they apply directly to what you are doing right now with your servitor.

As you will find out from watching "The Dog Whisperer", your pet must come to you when it is called. It must move aside when you order it to and it must stay put when you tell it to do so. Your servitor companion therefore must always move and do what you tell it, there can be no hesitation. When you are not interacting with your servitor companion, it must stay away and must be reprimanded if it keeps popping up when it is not expected. Your servitor then is one of the greatest teachers that you can have to help you focus your mind and control your personal intent.

But how do you make a servitor do what you want?

You make a servitor do what you want by focusing your mind, in this present moment, on what you want. For example let's say that you want your servitor to go from one end of the room to the other. To do this you need to focus on seeing your servitor go from one end of the room to the other, in this present moment, without effort or strain. It does no good for you to try to beg it to do what you say, it does no good for you to try and scream at it so that it does what you want, and it does no good for you to try and cry and whine to make it do what you want.

To get it to go from one end of the room to the other, focus your mind in this present moment on seeing it move from one end of the room to the other. Do not stress, do not make an effort aside from the effort required for you to focus your mind on this one particular thing. If you want your servitor companion to start dancing before you, visualize in this present moment that it is doing so, and then let it continue on its own. The trick is not effort but focus; see what you want to happen in your mind's eye and it will happen. When your servitor does something that you do not want, it is because in your own mind you are not clearly focusing on only, that is only, the one thing that you want. If as you focus on your servitor doing what you want, you are also thinking a bit about what you are going to do tonight, and also perhaps you are thinking that your servitor will not do what you want, that it is being stubborn, then you are not focusing on what you want but focusing on other matters.

A true and focused command, one that will be followed without reservation, must be focused like a laser. You focus completely on what you want without strain or effort and when this is done perfectly, your command is followed perfectly, without hesitation. As you focus your mind in this way, energy will naturally accumulate on your desire and intent. As the energy around your intent grows, your desire will be followed.

If for whatever reason you feel that your servitor companion is being rebellious, first and foremost realize that this is a problem that you have, not your servitor. If this is happening to you frequently, it is because you are not focusing your mind correctly on what you want and are perhaps making too much of an effort thinking that your servitor can somehow resist your mind, which it can't. I suggest that you:

- Study "The Dog Whisperer" a little more
- Practice focusing your mind on one particular thing to the exclusion of everything else. You can do this simply by closing your eyes when you have a quiet moment and try to focus your mind on one thing only. For example you could close your eyes and try to think of an apple and nothing else. As you do so you will notice many other thoughts intruding into your mind, just let these thoughts and impressions go and keep concentrating on your apple. With a little practice, your mind will get stronger and you will be able to narrow your focus like a laser.
- Stop trying so hard, your efforts should be directed towards focusing your mind, not in trying to will your servitor to follow your directions.
- Ignore your servitor. Since your servitor requires your attention and the psychic energy that you give it through this attention, banishing it from your mind for a while is a great way to recharge yourself and refocus your energies.

The final thing you can do if you feel like you have made a mistake, is that you can drain the life out of your servitor. Some might think that this is the ultimate disciplinary tool to threaten their servitor into compliance; either you do what I want or I take some of your life away. But I really want to get away from this point of view because it is a highly incorrect one. What I'm trying to say to you is that servitors do not go rogue, they do not defy you and rebel like some kind of evil Frankenstein beast or like an uppity spoiled child. A servitor is a thing created by you and gets its strength and life through your efforts. The servitor doesn't go rogue, your mind goes rogue. So control your focus and your intent and there is no problem.

But if for some reason you feel that you have made a mistake or that somehow your servitor is no longer in your control, then you can use this final technique to erase the existence of your servitor companion. What I will be showing you here is a technique to absorb the psychic energy and attention you gave this creature. This is true energy absorption; you are absorbing the energy that gives your thoughts subjective existence (when there is a small amount of this energy) or objective form (when there is a great deal of this energy imbued into them).

To do this, begin by calling your servitor to you. If for some reason you are not able to call your servitor to you because you feel that it is rebelling on you then in a quiet place where you can be by yourself bring your servitor's image into your mind's eye. If you're still having trouble with this then just use your servitor's name; think of it in your mind as you do the following;

- Breathe out in a quick manner, try to get rid of 80% of the air in your lungs.
- Breathe in slowly while you are maintaining the image of your servitor or the visualized name of your servitor in your mind.

- As you breathe in very slowly, imagine that your throat is very constricted, it is very hard for you to breathe in. As a result you begin to breathe in air through the palms of your hands, literally sucking air from the palms of your hands into the center of your being.
- As you suck in this air through the palms of your hands, imagine that with them you are also sucking in the very life force of the servitor in your mind's eye. You might wish to imagine that there is a white light, sort of like a luminescent fog, that is withdrawing from the servitor and is being sucked into the palms of your hands.
- After a very long in breath, sucking in the energy from your servitor, exhale quickly, emptying out the air in your lungs as much as possible.
- Once again inhale slowly, sucking in the life from your servitor through the palms of your hands. Feel the pressure of your pull, your suction force, as you pull in this energy, this luminescent fog energy, through the palms of your hands and into the center of your being.
- Continue this process until you feel that the presence of your servitor is dwindling, sort of like it's fading out from existence before you. Continue until your servitor is completely gone and you can't feel its presence anymore.

This process can take a bit of time, perhaps even a few days or weeks. Basically what you need to do is to perform the process above until you feel that the presence of your servitor is gone. Later that day or perhaps on a different day in the future, you might feel the presence of your servitor; perhaps like it's trying to get your attention somehow. If this happens then perform the same technique mentioned above until the presence of your servitor is gone. It is this kind of process that might continue for a little while, all depending on how powerful your servitor was to begin with; how much psychic energy you gave it.

Servitors/thought forms can never be truly destroyed; no thought can ever be destroyed after it has been created. Those that tell you that you can somehow dismantle a thought form truly don't know what they are saying. A thought is forever, but it is the conscious attention that we give it that transposes it into what we consider our vibrational frequency, our objective reality. By draining its life, the attention/psychic energy that we have given it, we are taking away that part of it that allows it to exist within this frequency that we call consensual reality. All thoughts continue to exist and continue to fulfill different probable realities in different systems; that includes every single thought that you have ever had. Your servitor will continue to exist and fulfill itself in its own way in realities that you might never be aware of. This is just one of the many aspects of your creativity, of your power as a creator. It will not though be able to interact with you in this dimension because you have taken its power away.

This then is the final step really, you give life and you have the power to take it away; at least within this probable universe that we call our objective and consensual reality. Create with care and take responsibility for these creations. But most of all have fun and try not to take things so seriously. Control your mind but explore your feelings and let the power inside you bring light, color, and magic to your life. Magic is all around you, you just have to let it out.

Chapter 6:
Maintenance and Care of Your Servitor Companion

This probably sounds like a really boring chapter. I suppose the title makes it seem like it's a car repair manual or something. But in reality it is a much lighter chapter than you would imagine. If you have a basic idea of what I'm talking about when I tell you to control the focus of your mind around your servitor, then you are basically covered.

Whenever we do something physically or mentally, in order to do the very best that we can, we need to focus completely on this one act. So for example if I am washing dishes, I need to focus on the act of washing dishes instead of spreading myself all over the place trying to multitask. I could for example wash dishes and think about what I'm going to get Aunt Betty for a Christmas present or I could also be thinking about all the stuff I've done during the day. I shouldn't then be too surprised when I make a mistake or two and break a dish. Focus is what allows me to do a good job.

In order to do a good job with your servitor, you need to focus on what you're doing. If you are telling it to go from one end of the room to the other, then you need to focus solely on this mental act. While you are charging your servitor, you need to focus on the effect of charging the servitor, not on what you are going to get your aunt for Christmas. In order to get your servitor to follow your commands correctly, all you need to do is to focus your mind on this thing that you are doing at the moment. That is the only trick; focus your mind on this present moment and on the one thing that you are doing, forget about everything else.

Aside from that, the maintenance and care of your thought form means "having fun with your servitor companion". Whenever you play and interact with your servitor, you are paying attention to it. This attention that you are giving to your servitor is what essentially charges it and develops its personality. The more fun that you have with it, the more laughs that you enjoy in its presence the better, because it is through these strong feelings and attention that you saturate it with the kind of energy that it needs to develop, grow, and maintain itself.

In order for you to get a good idea of what I'm talking about, I am going to describe a typical day with my servitor companion. I have had this servitor companion for a number of years now so it is quite strong and quite well developed. I'm changing its name and some of its attributes in order to protect the innocent as it were.

I have been out all day running errands, I am a bit tired and I am glad to be home. I am home alone, no one else to interact with on the human level but this is not a terrible thing; I do like my alone time.

Speaking of which as I walk through the door and head for the kitchen to make myself something to eat, Blue (my servitor companion) floats by upside down with a stupid smile on its face. "So much for being alone", I think. I "growl" at it but it just keeps floating by, saying something along the lines of," I'm a cloud." I ignore it as it floats by and disappears from my line of sight...but there is a little smile in the corner of my mouth.

I decide to clean up first, but I eventually do get to the kitchen and start cooking. As I do so, I start to relive the dramatic moments of my earlier outing; I must admit I do hate crowds. Nobody around to vent to, I'm home alone, so like most people that have a servitor companion, I start to vent out loud to seemingly no one in particular.

"Man, I hate being in crowded places," I flail my arms around a bit as I jabber on for extra emphasis. "I'm moving to the country!" Blue materializes on the counter, he is encased in what looks like a clear plastic beach ball, its little limbs stick out from the beach ball but they are encased in yellow rubber gloves and boots.

"Ha ha, I get it 'bubble boy'." Blue bounces off the kitchen counter like an out of control beach ball and disappears behind it. He crawls back up onto the counter and is carrying a little tiny chair in one hand and a whip and the other. He is whipping all around him trying to hold the evil crowds (I would imagine) at bay.

"Yeah well I wish I had that bloody chair, and definitely the whip earlier." Blue drops the whip and chair making like whatever he was trying to hold back was too much for him. He dives off the edge of the counter again and disappears. I roll my eyes.

He finally pops himself back up doing a chin up over-the-counter edge." You suck," it tells me with a big smile on its face. I laugh," well what would you know of large crowds you spoiled pain in the butt pooka."

Blue is standing now on top of the counter after having pretended to struggle for half a minute to get itself up. It has a really tiny little violin this time and begins to play it with a look of sadness and self-pity on its face. He looks so silly standing there playing and looking up at me, the look on its face is so ridiculous, and the whole situation is suddenly just so ridiculous to me, I mean here I am having a battle of wits with my imaginary friend and losing, that I start to laugh out loud. Blue laughs with me and I forget about my griping for a while.

I concentrate on my cooking and want to be alone for a while so blue disappears and I continue cooking with a smile on my face.

After having a good meal, I decide that I'm just going to watch TV. I plop myself down on the couch and begin watching a show I like. Blue is suddenly beside me, and quietly hangs out to keep me company.

"Maybe I should get a cat", I say with a smirk.

"Well, if you would rather rummage through kitty litter encrusted poop than have an intellectual conversation with me, go for it," Blue replies with its chin up in indignation.

I laugh and lose myself in the TV show. I absentmindedly pet him and he starts to purr, I laugh.

This is an example of an exchange I had with blue a little while back. Blue is the cute little creature that keeps me company and it was developed and designed by me so that we could have fun interactions. Generally speaking, blue can lift my spirits anytime that I have an interaction with it.

While I had a general idea of the kind of servitor companion I wanted, many of its personality traits developed on its own. It has become quite the comedian for example and seems to enjoy making me laugh as much as possible. It has also developed a superior attitude when it comes to certain things and can definitely be a snob at times.

To me the snobby attitude is part of the charm. Blue is constantly making me laugh and I let it get away with a lot because as you might be able to tell from the exchange above, the ultimate goal of his little show is to try and make me laugh. Do realize though that I never let it go too far, that is I am always in control and will let it go on only to the point that it is entertaining me. If at any time I feel that it is getting a little too mischievous, I will stop him in his tracks. I do this by either giving him a stern look and reprimand him or turn my attention away from him completely. This has always been all that is required to keep any of my servitors in line. When I finally call him back, Blue is usually all apologies backed up by giant Bambi eye cuteness.

If ever I get tired of my interactions with Blue, it goes away. Generally speaking, if I don't pay attention to it, it just sits around quietly keeping me company or it moves on to where I can't see it. There are times when I need to command it to go away because it is annoying me, and it disappears instantly. The trick is to always maintain a fine balance between giving it complete freedom and reining it in. With practice though this becomes a really natural process, and there is no feeling of a fake type of interaction. Blue is my pet in a way, it goofs around and does whatever it thinks will make me happy, and whenever it happens that it steps over the line as it were, I prod it back without hesitation. This is my servitor, it wants to develop and grow just like any thought will develop and grow, but it requires and appreciates my leadership because this allows it to have a very unique relationship and structure.

Blue has become quite complex and as a result knows a lot about many things. As part of its developing personality, it has developed a superior attitude when it comes to some things; Blue is essentially a snob. There are times when it even tries to talk down to me, and I let it do this because some of our interactions can become quite hilarious and fun. If it ever gets a little too much for me though, I send it packing and tell it to go away. That's always enough to keep it in line.

Am I afraid that Blue will turn on me somehow? Am I afraid that I am playing with fire as it were? Of course not!

Blue is mine, my creation. I gave him a kind of life through my energy and attention and I can take that energy and attention away if and when I choose.

The prevailing theory is that any thought form that develops enough (that is any thought form that is given enough psychic power and attention) will free itself from the maker's control. But this is a fallacy that is expounded by those that do not understand the underlying properties of thought within this dimension and those that do not understand the power of human intention. They believe that all powerful thought forms become alive over time and all of these thought forms go rogue as it were. But the reality is that thought forms cannot attain sentience within this dimension and no matter how powerful a thought form might be, it can never overcome the concentrated intent of even one human being. If this weren't the case then our planet would be overrun by wild manifested thought forms that controlled every facet of our lives.

While it is the case that some powerful thought forms are causing misery in the lives of some people, this happens because they do not believe in thought forms and therefore ignore any evidence to the contrary, or these people are not knowledgeable in matters of energy manipulation, and they have never been successful at controlling their subjective reality (which in and of itself, without the help from anyone, would give them all the knowledge and power that they need to overcome negative thought forms).

If you find yourself in this position then I would recommend my book "The Vampire's Way to Psychic Self Defense". In this book you will discover how to overcome negative subjective feelings and negative thought forms, and will discover that the true masters of the psychic realm are not rogue thought forms but Inorganic Beings which are often misidentified as negative thought forms.

PLEASE then have fun with your servitor creations! Have fun with your Servitor Companions! Let them show you through play and pleasure how to control your inner reality and your intent. Create with joy and freedom. Discover how wonderful your creative power is and how magical and beautiful this world can be.

Chapter 7:
Create a Servitor Advisor

Within the realm of servitor companions, there is certainly a near infinite diversity since you can essentially put together any kind of companion that you can imagine. There is for example a type of servitor companion that can be incredibly useful and as far as some are concerned, is the best kind of companion. The companion that I am speaking about is called a Servitor Advisor and depending on your personality and desires, it can be an indispensable creature to have around.

As the name suggests, servitor advisors are usually used as advisers on any topic imaginable. For example if you would like to learn how to play an instrument, or are a musician that spends a great deal of your time thinking about music and music composition, you can create a servitor advisor that would help you to learn and compose better music. If you are learning the martial arts or if you are a dedicated martial artist for example, you could create a servitor advisor that would help you understand key concepts and motivate you to practice and to develop correct form.

A servitor advisor can:

- give you advice
- correct mistakes
- disclose secret information
- keep you on task
- inspire, motivate

But can the servitor advisor be that smart?

Well, if you will remember what I have already mentioned about thought forms, there is no way that even a highly complex servitor advisor could know and access information like this. What is actually happening here has to do with the network connections that I mentioned in the first chapter.

What a servitor advisor does is that it inspires your inner psyche and creates a kind of scaffolding that allows you to access deep inner knowledge. In many ways you could say that a servitor advisor is a self-created muse.

When you create a servitor advisor you are first and foremost developing an image that will most likely have a direct connection to the kind of information that you seek. For example if you wish to learn about the martial arts, it's quite likely that you will create a servitor advisor that looks like an old martial arts master. In order to create this thought form, you need to focus a great deal of your attention and therefore your psychic energy into this image. As this image develops and becomes more real to you, the very coolness of it inspires you to develop it more and to pay more and more attention to it.

All of this attention and psychic force develops the network connection between you and it, as I had mentioned in the first chapter. It is this network connection that creates that scaffolding into your inner psyche.

Through your interactions, and its ever growing network complexity, you are able to delve deep into your psyche for intuitional information and this servitor advisor becomes the voice of this intuitional information. You are essentially doing all the work but it is your advisor that seems to be relating all of the information that you are acquiring thanks to your co-relation. Another way of saying this is that a servitor advisor allows you to fragment a small part of your personality which can then help you access and interpret internal knowledge. The fact that the servitor advisor is seen as an outside and separate entity is highly beneficial to your ego because it allows you to access and work with information that your ego would otherwise find intrusive and would therefore not allow you to access.

As the network connection between you and your servitor companion grows, your ability to access intuitional knowledge grows. This means that as your ability to relate with your servitor companion grows, it then is able to relate more and more powerful information to you. This information becomes clearer and easier for you to put into practice.

If you will remember back to the last chapter, my interactions with my servitor companion Blue were constantly making me laugh because I found them to be very witty. While my ego would like to take full credit and say that banter like this is a common part of my life with other people, it is indeed the case that I'm usually only this funny when Blue is around. That is Blue is my muse and it is because of our highly developed network connection that I am able to come up, through his actions and my own, with such funny material. Blue therefore is me and at the same time it is not me; as its creator I am able to interact with a truly individual thought form but I do so in a way that allows my psyche to play with itself as it were. Blue develops and grows through these interactions and my psyche develops and grows as it is able to control my companion and venture beyond just my ego self.

You must understand that this is not channeling. Channeling involves the contact with another conscious entity that is most likely no longer focused in physical reality. This on the other hand is essentially the exploration of inner knowledge through the creation of an artificially created window into my inner being. This window develops and grows the more that I use it and I can even adjust the kind of flow that I allow to go through it, just like a regular window. I can also close this window or completely dismantle it in the future if I choose.

To begin creating a servitor companion:

Start by trying to find an avatar/fetish that represents the kind of advisor that you are looking for. If you are looking for a servitor advisor to help you with your martial arts, you could for example create a servitor advisor that looks very much like the blind kung fu master that instructed Kwai Chang Caine. If you are wishing to learn or like to discuss things that have to do with computer science and programming, you could create a servitor advisor that looks just like a futuristic talking computer or android. Feel free to use any image that you like, and anything that you can find in cyberspace. As before, try to stay away from people that you know, have known, or are wanting to meet in the future.

Charge the servitor advisor just like you did with your servitor companion. When you get to step four though and you start interacting with your servitor, I want you to imagine that this is the time when your advisor begins to absorb all that knowledge that it will later use to talk to you and advise you whenever you need it. To do this I want you to imagine that as your servitor advisor is floating around your quiet room, it begins to absorb huge amounts of information into its personality. Imagine that as your servitor is floating in your quiet room it begins to absorb a kind of light, it begins to absorb light from all around its environment sucking it into itself sort of like a mini black hole; this light represents the information that it is sucking into itself. At the end of step four you should feel that your servitor advisor has absorbed huge amounts of information in the field that you have chosen for it.

When you are done, finish charging as usual following the other two steps left in the charging procedure.

When you have finished charging your servitor and it is fully functional, I personally suggest that you start by asking it simple questions at first. This is advisable because it will take a little time for you to develop that network connection that is all important in allowing you to access the kind of intuitional information that you need. Because of the visualizations that you did in step four, you won't need to take it easy with it for very long and you will soon be getting highly educated answers that will surprise you in their profoundness. The network connection is therefore very important and you develop this network by interacting with your servitor companion on a regular basis. Eventually you will be able to get truly specific answers to your questions, get advice on form or technique, and you will even be able to debate ideas and issues.

Chapter 8:
Servitor Lover?

Some I think will be asking this question. I mean it's a natural one right? You have this creature that you can create yourself. You can mold it into whatever image you desire, with any capabilities that you desire; you can essentially make it do and be whatever you want. Here you have a creature that through some effort on your part can be given a kind of life and as a result can develop its own type of personality.

Most importantly, if properly charged and maintained, this creature can actually be felt, and can touch you back!

Well the answer is of course yes; you can definitely create a servitor lover. A servitor lover is really just a variation on the servitor companion, in that it can specialize in one specific aspect of companionship.

Besides all the benefits stated above, remember that you can tell a servitor lover to go away when you are done with it, there are no recriminations and there is never any need for guilt because this being was created by you for this specific task; it is not a person, it is a servant thought form. Its growth is dependent on your growth; it grows through personal interactions with you which allow it to also participate in a variety of different types of new probable actions that it craves.

Do not therefore humanize your servitor; do not fill your thought creations with feelings of guilt, imposed beliefs about good and evil, repressed anxieties, or worries.

Your servitor companion/lover is here to allow you to grow through the development of your own ideas and the fulfillment of your personal values, which are most clearly expressed through the expression of your desires. In order to discover these values and in order to develop as an individual, you need to explore your personal desires and feelings. In other words this is no time for personal repression, think of your servitor lover as a form of emancipation.

The great thing about a servitor lover is that no one needs to find out about it. I actually always give the advice that you should keep all your servitors secret and talk about your doings with no one; you should neither give their names, talk about what they've done, or their capabilities. In order to show you what is possible, I sometimes share some of my stories, but unless you are doing something similar yourself, there is no need to tell anyone about your servitor lover. All your servitors should be kept secret.

There is a caveat to this, and I have seen this happen personally: a highly sensitive person will be able to see a servitor. They usually can't see the actual details of the servitor unless they are very powerful sensitives, but they can see the fact that there are strong energetic bundles that seem to be following you around. If you run into such a person then I would suggest that you share the fact that you have servitors but there is no need to say anything else.

Another possibility is that your servitor becomes so energized and detailed over time that it starts to become physically visible to some people. I wouldn't worry about this though because if someone actually sees your servitor out of the corner of their eye, as it streaks around a corner, they will most likely be so emotional about the fact that they saw this creature to begin with that they will completely forget about the fact that they actually saw a scantily clad nymph or male model!

Pros: no worries, no birth control, no recriminations, no prejudice, and no STDs.

Cons: People need people. Don't let your Servitor Lover (or companion for that matter) take over your life. They should be used for emancipation and the pursuit of greater pleasure, not as an excuse to become a hermit.

It is always very important to remember that you will not be creating a partner here, it will be a servant. This point can never be stressed enough because at no point is your servitor lover or companion to be treated as an equal. You are in charge always; your servitor is just that, a servant. This does not mean that you can't love your servitor as a servant, or that you can't allow your servitor to have a little free reign when it comes to certain things. Like I said before, it just means that you have to always remember that you are the creator and it is your creation, so you must take responsibility for that in every way possible.

Another thing that I would suggest to you is that you do not create a servitor lover from the image of someone that you know, have known, or plan to meet in the future. The reason for this is not because of some kind of dark control that you might develop over this person, or some other negative thing, like spirit possession or the like. My suggestion here has to do with that network that I told you about in chapter one.

Remember how I spoke of the ever-growing network both within your own psyche and within the thought form; this is the network that develops and expands itself every time you interact with your servitor. If you know or have already known the person whose image you want to use as your avatar/fetish, you can run into a little bit of trouble because you have already established a network within your psyche with that person. You know that person and have interacted with that person and have therefore created a network connection within yourself that is far more complex than you can possibly imagine. As a result, there might be repressed ideas and emotions and these can be projected onto your servitor.

If it's someone you plan to meet, someone you admire and perhaps want to get to know in the future intimately or otherwise, you will be creating a network connection that has everything to do with a servitor and nothing to do with an actual individual. This will greatly alter your relationship with that person in the future when you finally meet him or her, because you will be meeting a person whom you will identify with in a master to servant relationship, this can greatly alter and perhaps ruin a future relationship.

When you are creating a servitor lover therefore, remember to start fresh. Keep it light, think of it as a game, and explore your fantasies. You are not trying to re-create the one true love of your dreams; you are an adult exploring adult pleasures. Focus on the physical, explore the limits of what you consider to be beautiful and desirable and forget about anything having to do with mutual love. Mutual love is found between the hearts of individual people, as human souls connect. Not with your servitor, because your servitor has no heart or soul.

To begin then, start by thinking of your ideal lover from a completely physical point of view. Visualize the qualities that you want in this lover, whether it is big and powerful or fragile and gentle. Explore your feelings until you are satisfied that you have a rough idea of the kind of creature that would be most satisfying to you. The next step is to try and find an avatar/fetish that is the closest to your ideals. If you are a very talented artist, then you might want to create your own avatar/fetish. I would only recommend this to really good artist though because you must remember that physical detail is of the greatest importance here.

When looking for an avatar/fetish, I highly recommend you explore the cyber world. Whether you are looking for a male or female avatar/fetish, the cyber world is full of amazing images that you can use to your advantage. The world of manga is another example of an incredibly rich resource; I highly recommend that you do a little research in this area if you are not familiar with it. The great thing about manga is that if you find a character that you like, then you will have a huge collection of images that you can use in order to compile your avatar/fetish scrapbook or file. What's also great about manga is that many of these characters have little plastic collectible dolls that you can buy. These are absolutely perfect as avatar/fetishes.

If you are looking for something a little more realistic, then there is no reason why you could not use an image collection from a famous model or actor that you find absolutely ravishing (naked images are best of course). This is not a person that you probably have met or a person that you will meet in the future so there is no reason why you can't create a servitor lover that looks exactly like one of these famous people you admire.

Also don't forget to explore the world of fantasy; there is no reason why your servitor lover couldn't be an elf, a mermaid, a nymph, or whatever other magical being that you choose. Remember though that if you choose a creature like this for your servitor lover, that this servitor will not have the magical powers of such a creature, nor does it have to act in a way that resembles what this mythic being acts like in legend. This is a good thing when you want to have a vampire lover or the like ☺

Once you have chosen the image for your avatar/fetish, go about creating a little file with all the images that you think you will need in order to create the perfect servitor lover. If you can, try to get a doll or something similar if it is available. Once you have this avatar/fetish, you will need to charge your thought form in the same way that you charged your servitor companion.

With a servitor lover, physical detail is all important. Even if you are a highly kinesthetic person already, do remember that in order to feel these external sensations and inner pleasurable feelings perfectly, you will need a servitor lover that is capable of inducing these feelings. You must therefore make sure that you take a long time memorizing every detail of your avatar/fetish and that you take as much time as you need to instill every single physical detail that you can into your thought form.

In order to charge a servitor companion, in Step 4 of the process, I had said that you might want to take a week or more to make sure that you practice feeling your servitor with your imaginary hands. With a servitor lover this is a critical facet of its charging so I would suggest that you take as much time as you need in this step. You should be able to clearly feel your servitor, you should be able to feel your servitor in the way that you think it would feel like if you were to touch whatever part of its body that you are touching. In other words you have to make sure that during this process you become intimately aware of the feel of every single nook and cranny of your servitor lover.

Step four of the charging process will therefore take a little longer with a servitor lover for the reasons stated above. If you don't believe that you have the kind of physical detail and feeling that you want, do not be discouraged. As you begin to interact with your servitor lover, it will take on more and more detail because as I have said before, these interactions actually help to further charge your servitor and they can therefore greatly increase your thought forms physical details.

It is possible that you are feeling a little apprehensive about all this right now. Please don't. Believe it or not, desire is truly a big part of mental development. Desire imbues you with the impetus and energy necessary to create an objectified form or event so that you can derive pleasure from this creation and in this way explore your beliefs and values. Desire (this of course includes sexual desire) is also the impetus that our inner self uses to get us to work with energy and to develop our abilities as responsible creators.

A servitor lover might seem a little risqué to some but I suggest that you let go of some of your inhibitions and realize that this is a step towards your greater mental evolution, as you learn to manipulate your reality through the objectification of your desires.

There are some people that like to have a servitor companion that on occasion acts as a servitor lover. There are also those that like to have a separate servitor companion to interact regularly and a servitor lover for when the occasion arises. There are benefits to both systems:

- A servitor companion that is sometimes a servitor lover is good because the great degree of interaction that you have with it means that the servitor becomes quite detailed and powerful quickly. This is a good thing because the realistic nature of its physical makeup makes it a great servitor lover. Some also believe that the interactions that they have with them as a companion, makes them even more pleasurable lovers.
- A servitor lover that is only interacted with for intimate connections is quite a good idea for some because this allows the servitor lover to become very specialized in its makeup. While a servitor companion/lover can develop a type of personality that is

interesting and fun, it can also develop personality traits that make it unsuitable as a great servitor lover.

It will have to be your choice in this matter. Think about what you want from your servitor companions and lovers and see if one or the other fits the bill best. Remember also that you can completely alter the way that you are interacting with your current servitor and that you can even completely dismantle one (drain one) and start again if you like.

Interacting with your servitor Lover:

Now you might be thinking, "how is it that I'm going to...err, interactive with my servitor lover?".

Well, do you remember when I was petting my servitor companion Blue? At that time I didn't mention it but because of my distraction with the TV, I was not aware of how I was doing it. What I mean by this is that I wasn't sure if I was petting Blue imaginatively or if I was actually physically lifting my hand and touching 'Blue' the thought form.

You see this is how things go after a while with your servitor companions. There will be very little difference in your experience to let you know whether you are interacting with your servitor companion in your mind exclusively or whether you are quite physically interacting with it. This might seem odd but please d realize that all of our physical actions are essentially a mental construct. What I mean by this is that, those that practice this 'internal to external' magical worldview realized a very long time ago that all of our apparently external reality is just internal action that has certain seemingly physical characteristics in accordance with our personal world view and socialization.

Science has recently confirmed aspects of this by demonstrating that what we consider to be physical reality is in fact just neural interpretations of something weird that is happening 'out there'. It has also been able to prove that our mental capabilities are such that even physically imagined events can create similar neural connections to those that would be created by someone actually performing a physical act. In other words, a vividly imagined physical action is almost the same thing as actually doing it, according to your mind.

If you would like to further research this subject, then I suggest the book "The User Illusion" by T. Norretranders.

The work of Neuroscientist Alvaro Pascual-Leone, specifically this Times article:

http://content.time.com/time/magazine/article/0,91 71,1580438-1,00.html/

I would also recommend my book "The Occult Experience" available on Amazon Kindle.

Now this doesn't mean that there will be no physical interactions as such with your servitor lover. It just means that at certain moments, especially if you decide to use that technique called the 'servitor room' discussed in the next chapter, your interactions with your servitor lover will happen mostly in your mind and they will be just as valid within your mind as they will be physically. This will not be the case all the time, it will just happen sometimes, especially at first when you are developing and charging your servitor lover through interactions with it.

Generally speaking then, your first interactions with your servitor lover, after you have finished charging it, will involve purely mental and autoerotic practices on your part. At first, the image of your servitor will most likely be quite clear but it will be difficult for you to interact with it on a physical level alone. Through autoerotic practices you will be interacting with your servitor in a very powerful way by using its image to excite yourself sexually. As you continue in this kind of interaction, you'll develop a greater and greater ability to touch it within your mind's eye and to have it perform different things that you find stimulating.

As you continue with this practice, the vividness and realism of your servitor lover will increase very quickly. There will come a point when you will be able to completely relax physically because its image and the feel of its touch will seem so real to you. At this stage you will most likely still be directing every single action that it makes with your mind and you might still use autoerotic stimulation every once in a while. You will slowly begin to see a transition though, where you begin to increase the amount of physical stimulation (caressing, kissing, etc.) that you give your ethereal lover and decrease the amount of physical stimulation that you give to yourself. In other words the sexual interactions that you have with your ethereal lover will start to seem very physically real to you.

Note: there are many practitioners that only like to have interactions with their servitor lovers within their minds; inside the servitor rooms that they have created. They believe that the intensity of these purely mental interactions can far surpass mere physical ones and there is also a much greater flexibility as to what they can do with their lovers; such as having interactions in zero gravity, underwater, another planet, using different costumes and settings, etc.

Through these further interactions with your servitor lover, there will come a time when I like to personally say that the magic truly begins. This is the time when your servitor will seem to act in random ways that will catch you by surprise, that is it will begin to do things on its own and this will greatly increase your pleasure because it will truly begin to feel like you are interacting with a real living lover.

A servitor lover can become incredibly real because the sexual energy that you are using when you interact with it is very powerful. If you are diligent, and do not change your servitor lover often (which is something that some people tend to do) you will very quickly develop a very sensual and dynamic servant lover that you can use to increase your pleasure, reduce your loneliness, and explore the limits of your desires. It will even be the case that this servitor paramour will help you to become a better lover with 'real' people because it will introduce you to and help you develop different techniques that will turn you into an amazing lover.

Chapter 9:
Servitor Companion Room

With a servitor lover, a servitor advisor, and sometimes with a servitor companion you might have already realized that there is a gap between objective and subjective action. Remember when I talked about petting my servitor companion Blue? At that time I can honestly say that I could have petted him with my mind or I could have physically reached out and petted him with my hand, there is usually very little difference to me between one and the other.

The reason why there is this odd ability to interact with the servitor on a subjective and objective realm with equal facility is because these are creatures that bridge two realms. Certainly the biggest reason why we all create servitors to begin with is that they allow us to fulfill certain desires, but the truly amazing thing about them is that when we go about doing this, we begin to truly understand how it is that we shape our own reality. We follow a step by step procedure that allows us to take a subjective thought (or idea) and turn it into an objective reality.

A servitor of any kind is a powerful and well energized thought form. As we already know, a thought form is essentially no different from any other thought that you might have, except for the fact that our intense attention and emotions feed it psychically until its vibrations change, it becomes more solid, and is then able to interact with what we considered to be objective/physical reality. Since our entire world is the result of thoughts made manifest through deep subconscious psychic actions, the creation and the manipulation of thought forms allows us to truly become skilled 'conscious' creators.

Generally speaking, this physical universe that is all around us, this objective world that we interact with and consider quite real, is created in a type of automatic fashion. What I mean by this is that we are not really consciously aware of the incredible creative endeavor that we perform every single moment of every single day, and take all of it quite for granted. It is my belief, and the belief of many, that in this lifetime we are learning how to more consciously create through our thoughts, emotions, and focused attention.

A servitor then is an amazing creative exercise because it allows us to manifest some of our desires and at the same time it gives us a very good idea of how to develop this god like ability further, and completely alter all the facets of our lives. The servitor does this by showing us how a quite consciously created thought goes from being purely subjective and ethereal in form to a much more objective thing that can alter our physical world.

It is that bridge then, that movement from a mental thing to an objective thing that truly shows us the power and the magic deep within all of us. Since this bridge or gap is so important, it is a very good idea to create what I like to call "The Servitor Room".

The servitor room does not exist in physical reality, it is a place in the mind that you create in order to specifically interact with your servitor companion, advisor, or lover. If you have ever done any kind of meditation then you are most likely familiar with what I refer to as a room in your mind; this is the white room where all is possible, this is the 'room without walls'.

In this internal place, it is much easier to interact with a servitor companion, advisor, or lover because your imagination is literally unbound and your external sense data is replaced by internal sense data and construction that has a far greater facility. In this room you will be able to hear, see, feel, taste, and smell your servitor in a far more direct way. As a result your interactions become far more real to you and this can be very important because it allows you to interact and therefore charge your servitor with greater ease and power.

If you have created a servitor lover for example, it will be much easier for you to become intimate with it for the first time in this room. Even if your servitor lover is well charged and has a definite objective reality to you, it can sometimes be difficult to be intimate for the first time with your etheric lover because intimacy often times requires such deep physical sensations. In this internal room, you will be able to experience your servitor lover in a far more sensual way than you could in the objective world; at least for the first few times you get together.

Another great thing about interacting with your servitor in this internal room is that each one of these interactions helps to charge it. The reason for this is that each interaction in this room focuses so much attention on your servitor. In this room it is also a lot easier to further develop the physical look and fine detail of your servitor and as you focus on and develop your ability to touch it in this internal room, you also develop and expand your abilities to do the same in the physical objective world. In other words this room then truly becomes a bridge from the subjective into the objective as it helps to train your neural structure and it helps to charge your creations.

In order to begin to create your servitor room, all you need to do is to close your eyes in a quiet place where you will not be disturbed for a while. When you close your eyes, the first thing that you will probably notice is the back of your eyelids. What I mean is that if you have a quiet mind, without mental intrusions from other aspects of your day, your mind will be silent enough that you will only notice the light that shines through your closed eyelids. This usually looks like a big clear canvas of different colors depending on the lighting in the room that you are trying to meditate in.

So to begin then, find a nice quiet place where you can be alone for about 15 minutes to half an hour and try to relax your body as much as possible. I suggest taking three deep breaths and with each exhale focus on relaxing your body more and more. At the end of the third exhale, close your eyes and try and see this canvas that I spoke of. If you are having trouble seeing this canvas, because there seem to be so many thoughts superimposed over it, then I want you to open your eyes again and try to relax your body a little more. Try to forget the troubles of the day and focus your attention only on this present moment. Take another three deep breaths and once again close your eyes when you are done.

When you can close your eyes and can clearly see that blank canvas before you, try to superimpose the image of your servitor on it. Just like you created an image before you when you were charging your servitor originally, try to bring this image of your servitor before you now. If you have done a good job of charging your servitor then this will probably not be a big problem for you. Once your servitor is before you, try and have it move around that blank canvas in front of your eyes. This action will naturally heighten the meditative state that you are currently experiencing and before long you might begin to feel like this mental room has developed depth; that is, this internal room seems to have grown bigger and thicker in a way that is hard to explain with words alone.

As your servitor moves around your room, you might begin to experience more than just the feeling of depth within your room. You might also begin to experience certain colors and other hallucinations that seem to revolve within this room, deep inside your mind. I personally find that the best thing to do is to go with the flow of these hallucinations because they help to deepen my meditative state. It is most important though that you never lose sight of your servitor, that you always keep it as the most prominent feature in your mind's eye. This might be hard at first but the better the charge on your servitor the easier that this task will be, and the more time you spend developing this focus, the better the charge that your servitor will get.

When you feel that you have a real sense of being inside an internal room, and you have a clear image of your servitor within this room, I suggest that you consider adding furniture and other more distinctive features. You can essentially create any kind of room you would like, whether it is an old Victorian room with classical furnishings or whether you would like to create a garden so that your servitor can play.

There are two general ways you can develop the room:

1. You can leave your room completely blank so that it is always just a dark internal place where you and your servitor can interact completely alone. In occult circles this is usually referred to as the 'room without walls' and it is a highly effective way to focus solely on yourself and your interactions with your servitor.

2. The second method is to actually develop a room and in this way have a really fun and exciting place where you and your servitor can have many adventures together. It is also good to note that this room doesn't have to be a room, it can also be a place.

Both methods are quite legitimate and have their own pros and cons. It is up to you to decide what you enjoy most and what you feel most comfortable with. It could be that you might want to start with a blank room at first and then develop something a little more detailed as your feelings change. You may also want to create different rooms for different purposes. This is completely up to you and it really just involves a little extra time on your part. Do believe me though when I tell you that these servitor rooms are definitely worth it and make your interactions with your servitor companions far more powerful.

Conclusion

In order to describe our modern world we sometimes use the term 'the communication age'. We are very proud of ourselves, and rightly so, because we are now able to interact and share information in ways that our recent ancestors would not have believed.

Unfortunately the communication age in many ways is an oxymoron because even though we have increased our communicative power exponentially, we have also managed to isolate ourselves from our family and tribe. In times past, the community meant everything and we all took turns taking care of each other. Certainly this was not some kind of ideal world but there existed a type of community support. We all needed to interact with each other in order to stay well informed, healthy, and prosperous; we took turns taking care of each other.

In this modern 'communication age' there is no need for that physical community anymore; we can be half way around the world and still keep in touch with our family and those we consider part of our tribe. Most in the modern world lead lives where they interact more with electronic gadgets than they do with people. Sometimes even our closest friends are people that we interact with online only, and while some of these new communities can be highly lethargic, we still seem to require a type of physical interaction that is getting harder and harder to find.

Perhaps it is in this new modern world, this new communication age, this new 'cyber age', that we need servitor companions the most. There will always be a need for human to human contact and we should all make the greatest effort possible to propagate these kinds of relationships, but servitor companions can help to satisfy an incredibly powerful need within the human heart to interact with a self 'outside' our own. A servitor companion can first and foremost help us with the loneliness that is part of this modern existence.

Perhaps the loneliness of modern life is inevitable because as we grow intellectually we also require more time to ourselves in order to explore the great vastness of our new technological and mental potential. Servitor companions provide happiness, increased pleasure, company, advice, and a type of support that can help us to confront the vastness of our potential as individual human beings in this new technological age.

Servitor companions can also help us to develop that powerful intellect that we will need in order to participate fully within this fast moving modern world. Through their ability to help us rediscover our inner magic, servitor companions allow us to let go of our constricting one dimensional ego. With them we are truly free to have fun and play without any self-importance or self-limitation. With them we can explore the full depth of our true desires, and with them we are free to explore all our inner thoughts and ideas in an incredibly vivid new way; to entirely redefine our concept of 'I am'.

This ability to explore different aspects of our psyche without recrimination from others and from ourselves can greatly expand the scope of our personalities. It can allow us to develop many more aspects of ourselves that can make us more intelligent and can make us far more capable as individuals. The possibility of being far more self-contained, far more an island onto ourselves, can be an incredibly potent and empowering thing. Contrary to what some might imagine, this expansion of the self, thanks to our servitor companions, can actually make us far better at interacting with other human beings and teach us ways to develop healthy human relationships that empower us.

While some cultures around the world, especially in the Far East, find it easy to explore their inner realms, we here in the West still think that such things are childish and therefore regale them as taboo. It has been only recently, through great development in cyber space and the video gaming arena that we have really begun to explore the magical possibilities that are open to us through inner exploration and play. The servitor companion represents a bridge that allows us to truly objectify this inner magical reality that is currently available to us only through our toys, our games (video or otherwise), and our quickly expanding cyber culture. The servitor companion then represents the next step in the West's intellectual revolution; it represents our ability to truly merge with our inner reality and to expand beyond the limits of our personality. Servitor companions can become a blueprint of sorts that will help us develop and come to grips with advances in Artificial Intelligence and Virtual Reality.

Most importantly though, a servitor companion will show you that life is meant to be fun, to be a realm in which we enjoy ourselves immensely through the creation of our greatest fantasies. Our toys, our games, our silly little fantasies represent the inner need and the capabilities within all of us to live in magical and adventurous worlds.

A servitor companion is like a bridge to that inner magical world that most have lost contact with. They open us up to the realm of the magician's apprentice where all things have the possibility of coming to life and interacting with us, they are the rabbit hole that leads us into Wonderland, they are the doorways into the magic of our inner reality and the emancipation of our beings through great creativity, happiness, and play.

"Harvey and I have things to do...we sit in the bars...have a drink or two...and play the juke box. Very soon the faces of the other people turn towards me and they smile. They say: 'We don't know your name, mister, but you're all right, all right.' Harvey and I warm ourselves in these golden moments. We came as strangers - soon we have friends. They come over. They sit with us. They drink with us. They talk to us. They tell us about the great big terrible things they've done and the great big wonderful things they're going to do. Their hopes, their regrets. Their loves, their hates. All very large, because nobody ever brings anything small into a bar. Then I introduce them to Harvey, and he's bigger and grander than anything they can offer me. When they leave, they leave impressed. The same people seldom come back."
— Elwood P. Dowd

The mad Hatter asked, "Have I gone mad?" Alice replied, "I'm afraid so. You're entirely bonkers. But I'll tell you a secret. All the best people are."
— Alice in Wonderland

Made in United States
North Haven, CT
01 February 2023